MAKE A PACK YOUR WAY!

Building Bags to Haul Your Gear

ELSIE OLSON

CONSULTING EDITOR, DIANE CRAIG,
M.A./READING SPECIALIST

Super Sandcastle

An Imprint of Abdo Publishing
abdobooks.com

abdobooks.com

Published by Abdo Publishing, a division of ABDO, PO Box 398166, Minneapolis, Minnesota 55439. Copyright © 2020 by Abdo Consulting Group, Inc. International copyrights reserved in all countries. No part of this book may be reproduced in any form without written permission from the publisher. Super SandCastle™ is a trademark and logo of Abdo Publishing.

Printed in the United States of America, North Mankato, Minnesota
052019
092019

 THIS BOOK CONTAINS RECYCLED MATERIALS

Design: Tamara JM Peterson, Mighty Media, Inc.
Production: Mighty Media, Inc.
Editor: Megan Borgert-Spaniol
Cover Photographs: Mighty Media, Inc.; Shutterstock Images
Interior Photographs: iStockphoto; Mighty Media, Inc.; NASA/Wikimedia Commons; Shutterstock Images; Wikimedia Commons

The following manufacturers/names appearing in this book are trademarks:
Duck Tape®, Lunds & Byerly's®, Swingline®, Velcro®

Library of Congress Control Number: 2018967789

Publisher's Cataloging-in-Publication Data

Names: Olson, Elsie, author.
Title: Make a pack your way!: building bags to haul your gear / by Elsie Olson
Other title: Building bags to haul your gear
Description: Minneapolis, Minnesota : Abdo Publishing, 2020 | Series: Super simple diy survival
Identifiers: ISBN 9781532119767 (lib. bdg.) | ISBN 9781532174520 (ebook)
Subjects: LCSH: Outdoor recreation--Safety measures--Juvenile literature. | Survival skills--Juvenile literature. | Camping--Equipment and supplies--Juvenile literature. | Do-it-yourself work--Juvenile literature.
Classification: DDC 613.69--dc23

Super SandCastle™ books are created by a team of professional educators, reading specialists, and content developers around five essential components—phonemic awareness, phonics, vocabulary, text comprehension, and fluency—to assist young readers as they develop reading skills and strategies and increase their general knowledge. All books are written, reviewed, and leveled for guided reading and early reading intervention programs for use in shared, guided, and independent reading and writing activities to support a balanced approach to literacy instruction.

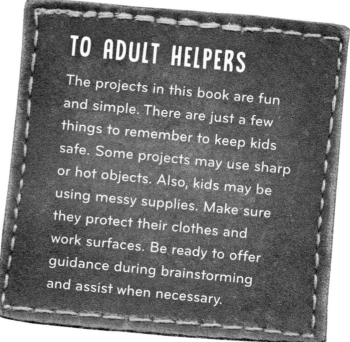

TO ADULT HELPERS

The projects in this book are fun and simple. There are just a few things to remember to keep kids safe. Some projects may use sharp or hot objects. Also, kids may be using messy supplies. Make sure they protect their clothes and work surfaces. Be ready to offer guidance during brainstorming and assist when necessary.

CONTENTS

BECOME A MAKER

A makerspace is like a laboratory. It's a place where ideas are formed and problems are solved. Kids like you create wonderful things in makerspaces. Many makerspaces are in schools and libraries. But they can also be in kitchens, bedrooms, and backyards. Anywhere can be a makerspace when you use imagination, inspiration, **collaboration**, and problem-solving!

IMAGINATION

This takes you to new places and lets you experience new things. Anything is possible with imagination!

INSPIRATION

This is the spark that gives you an idea. Inspiration can come from almost anywhere!

Makerspace Toolbox

COLLABORATION

Makers work together. They ask questions and get ideas from everyone around them. **Collaboration** solves problems that seem impossible.

PROBLEM-SOLVING

Things often don't go as planned when you're creating. But that's part of the fun! Find creative **solutions** to any problem that comes up. These will make your project even better.

SKILLS TO SURVIVE

Being a maker means being ready for anything. Your makerspace toolbox can even help you survive! People with survival skills learn to think fast and problem-solve. They find ways to stay safe and get help in **dangerous** situations.

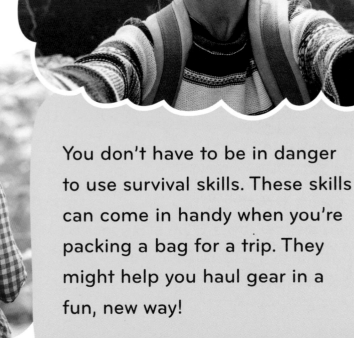

You don't have to be in danger to use survival skills. These skills can come in handy when you're packing a bag for a trip. They might help you haul gear in a fun, new way!

PROBLEM-SOLVE!
See page 26

BASIC NEEDS

Imagine you are lost in the woods or caught in a storm. What do you do? To survive, humans must make sure their basic needs are met. When you're building gear to help you survive, keep these basic needs in mind!

Air   **First Aid**   **Water**   **Shelter and Warmth**   **Sleep**   **Food**   **Help!**

IMAGINE A PACK

DISCOVER AND EXPLORE

Bags and packs are important survival gear. Think about all the packs you've seen or used. You might have a backpack for carrying school supplies, clothing, or sports gear. But packs can also carry food, water, and tools to help you survive. And with a little creativity, they can do much more!

GET INSPIRED!
See page 24

IMAGINE

If you could **design** a pack that could do anything, what would it do? Would it light up? Would it float or have wheels? Then, imagine a situation where you could use a pack to survive. Are you seeking shelter from a storm? Are you escaping **aliens** or pirates? Remember, there are no rules. Let your imagination run wild!

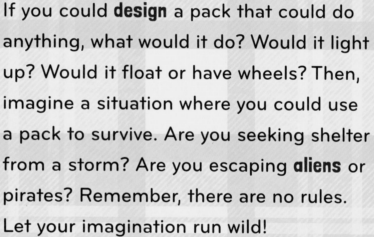

9

DESIGN A PACK

It's time to turn your dream pack into a makerspace marvel! Think about your imaginary pack and survival situation. How can the features of your pack help you survive? How could you use the materials around you to create these features? Where would you begin?

INSPIRATION

In 1984, NASA astronauts first used a pack that could fly them through space. The pack had 24 thrusters to power an astronaut's flight. The pack allowed astronauts to make repairs to a spacecraft without being connected to the craft!

COLLABORATE!
See page 28

BE SAFE, BE RESPECTFUL
MAKERSPACE ETIQUETTE

THERE ARE JUST A FEW RULES TO FOLLOW WHEN YOU ARE BUILDING YOUR PACK:

1. **ASK FOR PERMISSION AND ASK FOR HELP.** Make sure an adult says it's OK to make your pack. Get help when using sharp tools, such as a craft knife, or hot tools, like a glue gun.

2. **BE NICE.** Share supplies and space with other makers.

3. **THINK IT THROUGH.** Don't give up when things don't work out exactly right. Instead, think about the problem you are having. What are some ways to solve it?

4. **CLEAN UP.** Put materials away when you are finished working. Find a safe space to store unfinished projects until next time.

WHAT WILL YOUR PACK DO?

How will your pack help you meet your basic
needs? Knowing this will help you figure
out which materials to use.

Will it help you signal for rescue?
Then try using bright colors and reflective materials.

A waving flag could make you
easier for rescuers to spot!

PROBLEM-SOLVE!
See page 26

Will it protect you from monsters? Then give it armor. Maybe it has spikes!

IMAGINE

WHAT IF YOUR PACK NEEDED TO CARRY A PET CAT OR DOG? HOW WOULD THAT CHANGE THE MATERIALS YOU USE?

13

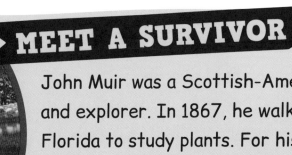

MEET A SURVIVOR

John Muir was a Scottish-American **naturalist** and explorer. In 1867, he walked from Indiana to Florida to study plants. For his trip, he packed only a comb, a bar of soap, and a few other items. Muir often slept outside and built fires for warmth.

Will it hide valuables from pirates? Then try **disguising** it as something else!

Rings, necklaces, and books are just a few items that can double as carrying vessels.

14

COLLABORATE!
See page 28

Will it provide shelter? Then use materials that can be arranged into a tent.

⚠ STUCK?

YOU CAN ALWAYS CHANGE YOUR MIND IN A MAKERSPACE. IS YOUR DISGUISED PACK TOO OBVIOUS? TRY TURNING IT INTO SOMETHING YOU COULD HIDE UNDER YOUR CLOTHES.

15

BUILD YOUR PACK

Packs are **containers**. That means they must be hollow. Look around for hollow objects that could form the structure of your pack.

SEARCH YOUR SPACE

The perfect shape might be in your kitchen cabinet, garage, or toy chest. Search for materials that might seem surprising!

GET INSPIRED!
See page 24

SUPER SMALL

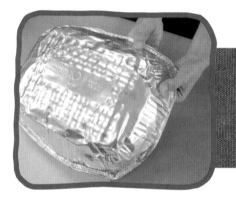

TIN CONTAINER

POCKET

CLASSIC PACK

FOIL PAN

POPCORN TIN

BIG & BULKY

BUCKET

CARDBOARD BOX

CONNECT YOUR PACK

Will your pack be **permanent**? Or will you take it apart when you are finished? Knowing this will help you decide what materials to use.

TOTALLY TEMPORARY

STRAIGHT PINS

CHENILLE STEMS

MAGNETS

BRASS FASTENERS

COLLABORATE!
See page 28

IMAGINE

WHAT IF YOUR PACK WERE GOING TO BE WORN BY A SHARK? HOW WOULD THAT CHANGE ITS LOOK?

A LITTLE STICKY

STAPLES

MOUNTING TAPE

SUPER STICKY

HOT GLUE

DUCT TAPE

DECORATE YOUR PACK

Decorating is the final step in making your pack. It's where you add **details** to your creation. How do these decorations help your pack do its job?

STYLE & FUNCTION

CRAFT FOAM

CARD STOCK

IMAGINE

WHAT IF YOU NEEDED TO SURVIVE IN THE SNOW? HOW WOULD THAT CHANGE YOUR PACK?

ALUMINUM FOIL

CHENILLE STEM AND BELLS

GET INSPIRED!
See page 24

KEEP IT CLOSED

STRAP IT ON

HOOK-AND-LOOP TAPE

BUTTON AND YARN

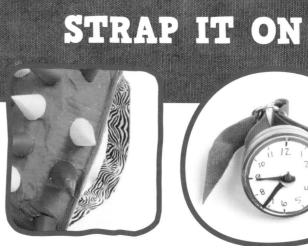

DUCT TAPE

LEATHER

NYLON WEBBING STRAP

21

HELPFUL HACKS

As you work, you might discover ways to make challenging tasks easier. Try these simple tricks and **techniques** as you build your pack!

To make a backpack flap, fold a plastic bag into a rectangle. Cover it with duct tape.

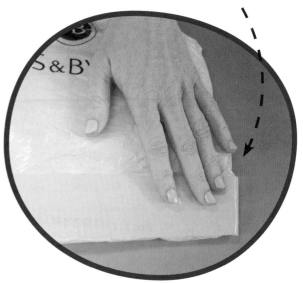

Put a tin inside a plastic bag. Cover the bag with duct tape to create the pack's shape. Then remove the tin from inside the bag.

Bend a foil pan into any shape you want.

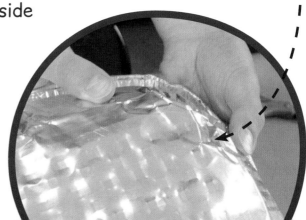

PROBLEM-SOLVE!
See page 26

Use a piece of string, drinking straws, and wooden dowels to create **collapsible** poles.

Braid three pieces of twine together for a sturdier strap.

Thread a leather strap through two key rings to make an **adjustable** wristband.

⚠ STUCK?

MAKERS AROUND THE WORLD SHARE THEIR PROJECTS ON THE INTERNET AND IN BOOKS. IF YOU HAVE A MAKERSPACE PROBLEM, THERE'S A GOOD CHANCE SOMEONE ELSE HAS ALREADY FOUND A SOLUTION. SEARCH THE INTERNET OR LIBRARY FOR HELPFUL ADVICE AS YOU MAKE YOUR PROJECTS!

GET INSPIRED

Get inspiration from the real world before you start building your pack!

LOOK AT PACKS

Look at backpacks, bags, suitcases, and other carrying cases. What features do you notice? How could you use some of these features in your pack?

LOOK AT WILDLIFE

Many animals have features that help them survive. Porcupines have spines that scare off predators. Some poisonous insects are brightly colored to warn animals not to eat them. Muskrats have **waterproof** fur to keep them warm and dry.

LOOK AT OUTDOOR GEAR

Outdoor gear might have features you could borrow for your pack. Some sleeping bags and coats come in tiny compression sacks. Raincoats and umbrellas are waterproof. Flashlights and headlamps are very bright and can attract attention. Winter jackets are filled with feathers to keep their wearers warm.

PROBLEM-SOLVE

No makerspace project goes exactly as planned. But with a little creativity, you can find a **solution** to any problem.

FIGURE OUT THE PROBLEM

Maybe your tent poles keep slipping and won't stand up. Why do you think this is happening? Thinking about what may be causing the problem can lead you to a solution!

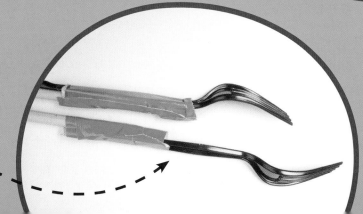

SOLUTION:
ATTACH FORKS TO THE ENDS OF YOUR POLES SO THE POLES CAN GRIP SOFT GROUND.

SOLUTION:
USE CLAY OR PUTTY TO MAKE THE POLE ENDS STICK TO HARD GROUND.

BRAINSTORM AND TEST

Try coming up with three possible **solutions** to any problem.
Maybe the straps of your armored pack keep breaking.
You could:

1. Use a different material for the straps.

2. Use a stronger connecting material to attach the straps to the pack.

3. **Adjust** the shape of the pack so it fits on your head and doubles as a helmet!

ADAPT

Still stuck? Try a different material or change the **technique** slightly.

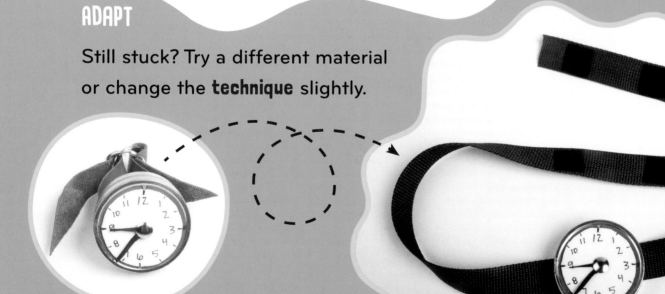

COLLABORATE

Collaboration means working together with others. There are tons of ways to collaborate to create a pack!

ASK A FELLOW MAKER

Don't be shy about asking a friend or classmate for help on your project. Other makers can help you think through the different steps to building a pack. These helpers can also lend a hand during construction!

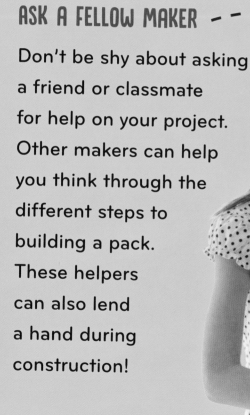

ASK AN ADULT HELPER

This could be a parent, teacher, grandparent, or any trusted adult. Tell this person about your pack's most important function or feature. Your grown-up helper might think of materials or **techniques** you never would have thought of!

ASK AN EXPERT

Someone who sells outdoor gear can tell you what materials outdoor packs are made of. A park ranger or **naturalist** can inform you about how to stay safe in different outdoor conditions.

29

THE WORLD IS A MAKERSPACE!

Your pack may look finished, but don't close your makerspace toolbox yet. Think about what would make your pack better. What would you do differently if you built it again? What would happen if you used different **techniques** or materials?

IMAGINATION

INSPIRATION

COLLABORATION

PROBLEM-SOLVING

DON'T STOP AT PACKS

You can use your makerspace toolbox beyond the makerspace!
You might use it to accomplish everyday tasks, such as organizing
your closet or studying for a science quiz. But makers use the
same toolbox to do big things. One day, these tools could help
design robots or clean up the world's oceans. Turn your world
into a makerspace! What problems could you solve?

GLOSSARY

adjust – to change something slightly to produce a desired result. An object is adjustable if it is designed to be used in more than one way.

alien – a being from outside Earth.

collaborate – to work with others.

collapsible – able to fold into a smaller shape.

container – something that other things can be put into.

dangerous – able or likely to cause harm or injury.

design – to plan how something will appear or work. A design is a sketch or outline of something that will be made.

detail – a small part of something.

disguise – to change the appearance of to prevent recognition.

naturalist – someone who studies plants and animals in the wild.

permanent – meant to last for a very long time.

solution – an answer to, or a way to solve, a problem.

technique – a method or style in which something is done.

waterproof – made so that water can't get in.